DATE DUE

APR 0 3 2002	NOV 1 8 2010
	MAY 2 8 2011
MAY 0 2 2002	JUL 0 6 2011
APR 2 8 2003	NOV 2 8 2011
MAR 2 2 2004 003	JUN 29 2012
MAR 2 2 2004	
JUN 0 9 2004	APR 0 6 2012
NOV 2 0 2004	MAR 2 7 2013
OCT 1 6 2006	MAR 0 3 2014
DEC 2 6 2007	APR 0 6 2015
DEC 0 1 2008	NOV 1 2 2019
MAR 0 9 2009	DEC 1 8 2019
OCT 2 2 2009	
DEC 2 9 2009	

Demco

The Sun

Experts on child reading levels
have consulted on the level of text and
concepts in this book.

At the end of the book is a "Look Back and Find" section
which provides additional information and encourages
the child to refer back to previous pages
for the answers to the questions posed.

Angela Grunsell trained as a teacher in 1969.
She has a Diploma in Reading and Related Skills
and for the last five years has advised London
teachers on materials and resources.

Published in the United States in 1985 by
Franklin Watts, 387 Park Avenue South, New York, NY 10016

© Aladdin Books Ltd/Franklin Watts

Designed and produced by
Aladdin Books Ltd, 70 Old Compton Street, London W1

ISBN 0 531 10027 8

Library of Congress Number:
85-50512

Printed in Belgium

FRANKLIN · WATTS · FIRST · LIBRARY

The Sun

by
Kate Petty

Consultant
Angela Grunsell

Illustrated by
Mike Saunders

Franklin Watts
New York · London · Toronto · Sydney

What is the Sun? The Sun is a ball
of burning gases spinning through space.
It is a million times bigger than the Earth.

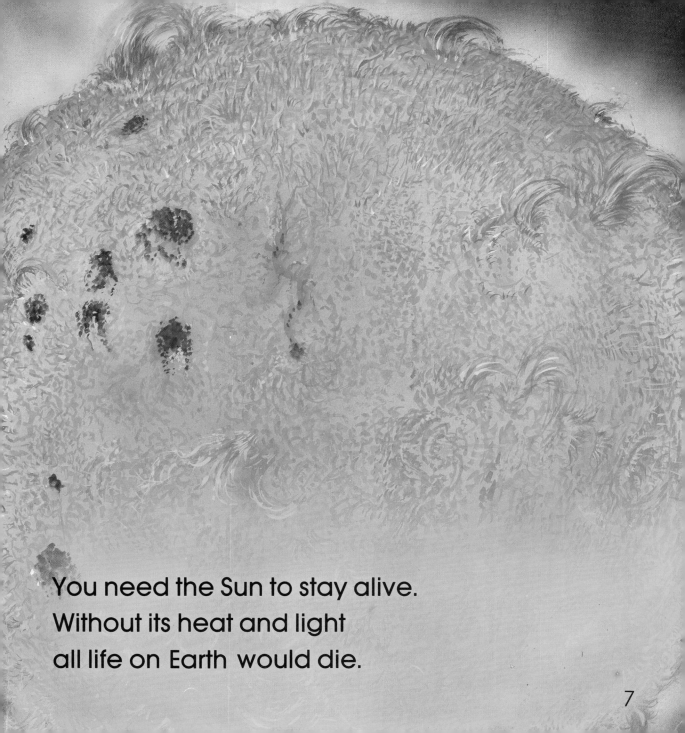

You need the Sun to stay alive.
Without its heat and light
all life on Earth would die.

7

The Sun is a star, like the other stars
you see in the sky at night. There are at least
100,000 million stars in our galaxy.

The Sun is our nearest star, even though
it is over 90 million miles away. It would take
a spaceship ten years to travel that far.

10

The Sun is not solid.
It is made up entirely of burning gases.
The Sun is hottest in the middle, where
the temperature is about 14 million°C.

Even on the outside, the temperature
is 6000°C. The Sun's surface changes
all the time. The violent flares are
millions of miles high. The dark spots
show where it is cooler.

Do you know what the Solar System is?
It is the group of planets and moons
that circle the Sun.
The Sun is at the center of the Solar System.

The path each planet takes
is called its orbit. The planets are held
in their orbits by the pull of the Sun's gravity.
Without it, they would spin off into space.

As the Earth travels around the Sun it also spins like a top. One complete turn takes 24 hours. Daytime is when your part of the world faces the Sun. Nighttime is when it turns away.

The Sun seems to rise in the east
and set in the west. Really, it is the Earth
that is moving, not the Sun.

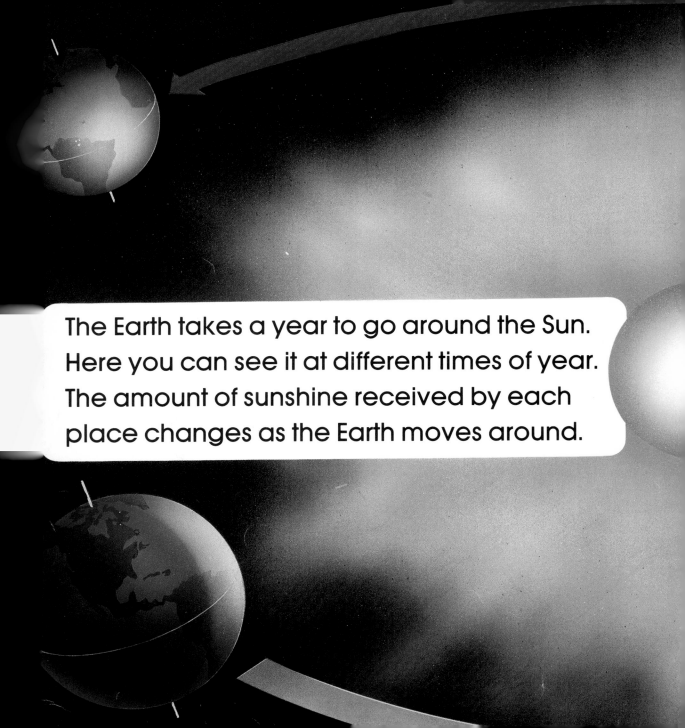

The Earth takes a year to go around the Sun.
Here you can see it at different times of year.
The amount of sunshine received by each
place changes as the Earth moves around.

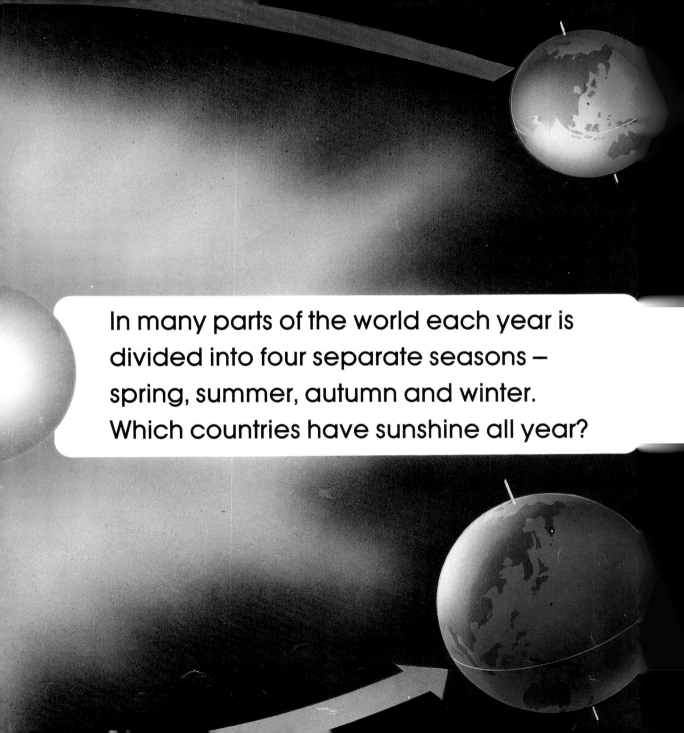

In many parts of the world each year is divided into four separate seasons – spring, summer, autumn and winter. Which countries have sunshine all year?

The Sun gives us light to see by, even when it is hidden by clouds. Shadows are formed when things block the path of the Sun's light.

Sunlight looks white, but the white light
is made up of many colors. You can
see these colors in a rainbow. The sunlight
is broken up as it passes through the raindrops.

The Sun gives out heat as well as light.
If you direct sunlight through
a magnifying glass onto paper,
the heat is magnified and can start a fire.

The house in the picture has glass solar panels
in the roof. Water for the whole house is
heated by the Sun. Infrared rays from the Sun
carry heat. Ultraviolet rays give you a suntan.

Light and heat are two sorts of energy
that come from the Sun.
Plants need sunlight to grow. We get
energy from plants when we eat them.

Coal is "buried sunlight."
It is made from plants that have rotted for millions of years. The energy we get by burning coal has been stored up for all that time.

Electricity can be made from sunlight. Satellites use this sort of power. Each square solar cell contains chemicals. An electric current is set up when light shines on them.

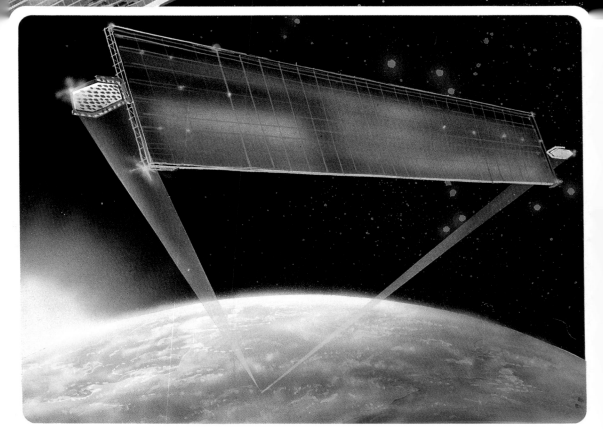

In the future giant satellites may be able to collect solar energy on a large scale and beam it back to Earth.

Stars do not shine forever. Astronomers have seen how old stars cool down and expand to become "red giants."

In millions of years' time this will happen to our Sun. People from Earth will have to search the stars for another place to live.

Look back and find

Why can't you see the stars in the daytime?
*The Sun is much closer to us than the stars,
so its light is far brighter than starlight.
You can only see the stars when the Sun
is out of sight.*

How far away is the Sun?

What is your normal body temperature?

How hot is boiling water?
Water boils when it is heated to 100°C.

How hot is the Sun?

What are the colors of the rainbow?
*Red, orange, yellow, green, blue, indigo,
violet — in that order.*

Do you know another name for the band of
colors in a rainbow?
A spectrum.

Why should you NEVER EVER look at the Sun through binoculars?
Because their lenses magnify the heat as well as the light and you could be blinded.

Can you see infrared rays and ultraviolet rays?
No, they are invisible to us.

What are two sorts of energy that come from the Sun?

Why is coal like "buried sunlight?"
Because the energy from the Sun stored in the plants when they were growing millions of years ago is still there in the coal today.

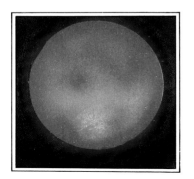

How can astronomers predict what will happen to the Sun in millions of years?
They have seen what happened to older stars.

What happens when a star grows old?
It expands and cools down. In the end the outer layers of gas drift away leaving the small white core of the star.

Index

PRINTED IN BELGIUM BY

INTERNATIONAL BOOK PRODUCTION